THE CHANGING SCENE OF
MERCHANT
SHIPPING

THE CHANGING SCENE OF
MERCHANT
SHIPPING
A PHOTOGRAPHIC SURVEY

DAVID HUCKNALL

The
History
Press

Cover Illustrations
Front: CMA CGM *Strauss* with a Hapag Lloyd vessel. (S.C.H. Hucknall)
Back: *Arklow Dawn*. (Author collection)

First published 2014

The History Press
The Mill, Brimscombe Port
Stroud, Gloucestershire, GL5 2QG
www.thehistorypress.co.uk

British Library Cataloguing in Publication Data.
A catalogue record for this book is available from the British
Library.

ISBN 978 0 7524 9339 8

Typesetting and origination by The History Press
Printed in Great Britain

CONTENTS

ACKNOWLEDGEMENTS

It gives me great pleasure to acknowledge the help and support given to me in the preparation of this book. I am particularly grateful to my wife Susan, who not only typed the manuscript with efficiency and accuracy, but also accompanied me on most of my ship-photography excursions.

I am also very grateful to Michael McKenna, who not only lent me his Nikon camera 'for as long as it was needed', but also provided me with some of his own excellent photographs.

Finally, I should like to thank ABP Southampton for providing me with a simulation of the port's new container berth (SCT5) and its facilities.

INTRODUCTION

An earlier book (*Merchant Shipping: 50 Years in Photographs*) reflected the contemporary scene from the early 1960s until the start of the 2000s. During this period, the use of containers to transport goods had increased markedly and cargo that had previously been shipped in 'loose form' was transferred to containers.

With both systems, loading and unloading are critical factors that determine the time a vessel spends on a berth. With traditional break/bulk vessels, relatively small hatches meant that a ship–dock transfer rate of about 18 tonnes/hour was typical and it was not unusual for a ship to be in port for several days. In contrast, the container-vessel rate was 370 tonnes/hour, resulting in an average of 1.2 days alongside (J.E. de Min, 'Navigating the Global Network Changes of the Ocean', BT Infonet). Probably as a consequence of factors such as this, by 2002, container ships accounted for 25 per cent of all new-vessel tonnage ordered.

A further advantage of containerisation is that the 'box' used can be appropriate to the cargo. Bananas, for example, are transported in containers chilled to exactly 13°C. As well as 'boxes' (e.g. TEUs (Twenty foot Equivalent Units)), 'flat tracks' (open to the elements) may be used. Tank containers can convey liquids as diverse as milk and corrosive chemicals.

The author's earlier book showed shipping (including container ships) up to the early 2000s. At the time, the size of container ships was gradually increasing in response to economic growth worldwide. For example, vessels built around the early 2000s had capacities of up to 5,000 TEUs. In the present decade, post-Panamax container ships (too large to go through the Panama Canal) have capacities of the order of 14,000 TEUs and the neo-post-Panamax vessels on order or under construction have a capacity of up to 18,000 containers. Ships such as these are designed for super-slow steaming at about 16 knots for greater fuel economy on the Asia–Pacific routes.

However, the shipping industry may be facing difficult times once again as 'economic woes across the world cause a sharp contraction in container trade'

(*The Telegraph*, 14 August 2012). The report indicated 'incredibly depressed' vessel rates after owners had 'overestimated' the buoyancy in Chinese exports.

Nevertheless, necessitated by the growth in container ships already mentioned, significant construction projects have been undertaken by port and harbour authorities. For example, ABP Southampton is constructing a 500m-long berth SCT5 (formerly Berths 201/202 – see *Merchant Shipping: 50 Years in Photographs*) capable of handling the world's largest container ships. Similarly, in competition with Southampton and Felixstowe, DP World (one of the largest marine terminal operators in the world) has planned the London Gateway Terminal at Thurrock. With six berths and the capability to handle ULC (Ultra Large Carrier) ships, it is planned to use automated container-handling systems to significantly reduce the time a vessel spends in port.

This book is a collection of photographs mainly covering the years since 2000, while making reference to earlier decades. Although ships in Southampton play a very large part, the ports of Vancouver and Hamburg are also included, as is the port of Abidjan in the 1980s.

Finally, as an indication that it is not just container-carrying vessels that are growing greatly in size, it was announced in September 2013 that P&O had ordered the cruise liner *Britannia* from Fincantieri's Monfalcone yard. At a cost of £500 million, it will carry 3,600 passengers and weigh 141,000gt.

1

CONTAINER SHIPS

The Mediterranean Shipping Co. S.A. (MSC) was founded in 1970 by Gianluigi Aponte. The *Rafaela* (1962; 11,090gt, 20,276 summer dwt) was the second ship acquired. She is seen here in the early 1980s at Berth 202 at Southampton. She was broken up in India in 1989. (Author collection)

Note: The reconstruction of Berths 201/202 will enable the port to accommodate the current generation of large container vessels at their loaded draught, providing 500m of quay with 16m depth alongside.

At the Port of Abidjan on 16 May 1983 were the vessels *Family Fotini* (1981; 16,119gt; IMO (International Maritime Organisation) 811334), *Margarethe Maersk* (1975; 16,119gt, 17,270 summer dwt) and the Pakistani *Tarbela* (1968; 9,739gt, 13,544dwt). The *Margarethe Maersk* was carrying a large number of containers on her deck. (Author collection)

Opposite top: The CMA CGM *Margrit* (2012; 141,635gt, 140,570 summer dwt; IMO 9465318) in MSC colours is seen at Berth 204 in Southampton on 30 June 2013. Built by Hyundai, Ulsan, she is owned by E.R. Schiffahrt, Hamburg. Her maximum TEU capacity is 13,102 (8,921 at 14 tons) and 1,600 reefers. (Author collection)

Opposite bottom: Off Hythe Pier and inbound for Southampton's Western Docks on 28 December 1980, was the Norwegian American Line vessel *Tanafjord* (1977; 7,000gt). As can be seen, it was common practice in the early 1980s to carry some containers as deck cargo. (Author collection)

The general cargo ship *Songkhla* (1977; 16,100gt; 23,314dwt; IMO 7526912) is seen at the Port of Abidjan on 26 December 1981. She had, at the time, a significant deck cargo of containers. Surviving until the late 1990s, her status is now recorded as 'dead'. (Author collection)

The *Usambara* (1983; 26,345gt) was built by A.G. Weser, Seebeckwerft (hull 1416). She had a capacity for 1,346 TEUs and 100 reefer plugs and is seen, dressed overall, at Abidjan, having completed her maiden voyage. She appears to still be trading as the MSC *Normandie*. (Author collection)

The *Australian Venture* (1977; 44,154gt, 39,454 summer dwt; IMO 7416911) was built for ANL by Bremer Vulkan, Vegesack, and had a maximum capacity of 1,700 TEUs. ANL was sold by the Australian government in 1989 and in 2006 the *Australian Venture* (as the MSC *Nuria*) was sold for demolition in India as 'a bucket of bolts'. (Author collection)

Seen at Berth 205, Southampton, on 26 February 1978, was the *Cardigan Bay* (1972; 47,442gt, 58,889dwt). Originally owned by Ocean Transport and Trading Ltd within overseas Containers Ltd. In October 1982, management was changed to P&O Containers Ltd. She worked the Northern Europe–Far East container service. (Author collection)

Built by Chantiers de l'Atlantique, the *S.A. Winterberg* (1978; 52,615 gt, 50,819 summer dwt; IMO 7422192) is seen here at Southampton. Formerly the *Transvaal*, she had a maximum TEU capacity of 3,090 and 964 reefers. Subject to frequent name changes, the name *S.A. Winterberg* was last reported in December 1992. (Author collection)

Jervis Bay (1992; 50,350gt, 59,283dwt; IMO 9005534) is seen at Berth 205 in Southampton on 12 April 1993. The vessel was managed by Blue Star GmbH. She retained her name until August 2009 and is now the MSC *Almeria*. (Author collection)

On 24 November 1991, NYK's full container ship *Katsuragi* (1990; 50,437gt, 59,418dwt; IMO 8910419) is shown leaving Berth 205 at Southampton. Behind the tug, at B204, EAC's *Toyama* can be seen. (Author collection)

At 12.50 p.m. on 8 June 2011, the NYK *Olympus* (2007; 98,799gt, 99,563dwt; IMO 9313987) was outward bound from Southampton, assisted by the tug *Svitzer Bristol*. Her capacity is 9,120 TEUs and 800 reefer TEUs. (Author collection)

Jacques Sade created CMA in 1978 as an intra-Mediterranean liner service. In 1996, CGM (a French state-run company) was sold to CMA and the company CMA CGM was formed. Here CMA's *Ville de Vesta* (22,667gt, 33,952dwt) is shown leaving Le Havre on 17 September 1988. (Author collection)

A modestly sized container ship, the NYK *Minerva* (1995; 29,383gt, 34,625dwt; IMO 9110951) was at Berth 204, Southampton, on 27 September 2000. With a capacity of 2,959 TEUs and 260 reefer points, she became the ANL *China* in 2002 and the *Maersk Portland* in 2007. She now appears to be the *Hammonia Caspium*. (Author collection)

Port-side to Berth 205 at Southampton is the NYK *Canopus* (1998; 76,847gt, 82,275dwt; IMO 9152296). She was owned by Zodiac Maritime. Built at Mitsubishi H.I.'s Nagasaki shipyard and engineering works, she could carry 6,208 TEUs and had 500 reefer points. (Author collection)

The OOCL *China* (1996; 67,625dwt; IMO 9108178) was a post-Panamax container vessel with a capacity of 5,344 TEUs. She was built by Samsung Shipbuilding and Heavy Industries, Goeje, and is now owned by Box Ships Inc. She is seen here, unusually, at Berth 107/108 at Southampton. (Author collection)

The accelerating increase in container-ship size is reflected in this view of CMA CGM *Voltaire* (2001; 73,172gt, 79,559dwt). With a total container capacity of 6,446 TEUs (3,398 as deck cargo, 3,048 below deck and 500 reefer points), she was owned by NSB Niederelbe Schiffahrt and launched as *Buxcoast*. (Author collection)

At Berths 205/206 at Southampton were the post-Panamax container vessels OOCL *Shanghai* (1999; 66,289gt, 67,584dwt; IMO 9198111) and OOCL *Los Angeles* (2000; 66,289gt; IMO 921169). Their container capacities were 5,770 and 5,514 TEUs, respectively. In April 2000, OOCL celebrated the naming of the two vessels. (Author collection)

A ship with an eventful career, this shows a view of the P&O *Nedlloyd Genoa* at Southampton. She was built in 1998 by Kvaerner Warnow Werft GmbH, Warnemünde. In December 2002 she was involved in a collision with the MT *Ebro* on the Elbe between Buoys 78 and 80. In January 2006, she was involved in an incident that resulted in the loss of cargo containers overboard. She was renamed *Maersk Phuket* with A.P. Møller, Singapore, as owner in February 2006 (Author collection)

Ben and Ellerman Line formed Ben Line Containers and introduced 'Third Generation' 2,804-TEU vessels. Shown here, astern of Hapag Lloyd's *Hamburg Express* (1972; 58,088 gt; 2,950 TEUs), is Ben Line's *City of Durban* (1978; 53,790gt), photographed at Southampton Container Terminal. (Author collection)

In 1974, Møller took delivery of its first container ship. It had a cargo capacity of 1,800 TEUs. Here, a later Maersk Line ship *Svendborg Maersk* (1998; 91,560gt, 110,387dwt; IMO 9146467) is seen at Berth 205, Southampton, in the early 2000s. Her capacity was 7,226 TEUs with plugs for 817 reefers. (Author collection)

A further development of Hapag-Lloyd's container ships was the *Bonn Express* (1989; 35,919gt, 45,977dwt; IMO 8711368). She was a product of HDW AG (hull 235) and had a TEU capacity of 2,803 (max.) and 154 TEU reefer containers. (Author collection)

At Berth 204, Southampton, is the *Sandra Blanca* (1994; 60,117gt, 63,014dwt; IMO 9074042). Formerly the NYK *Vega*, she had a capacity of 3,794 TEUs (4,743 max.) and 400 reefer points. She is now the MSC *Messina*. (Author collection)

After the French container shipping company CMA CGM was formed in 1996, the *Ville d'Antares* (1997; 40,268gt, 49,200 summer dwt; IMO 9157650) was pictured at Southampton with the joint company identified on her hull. This vessel had a maximum capacity of 3,961 TEUs (2,807 at 14t) and could also service 150 reefer TEUs. (Author collection)

Launched as the *Oriental Fortune* (1985; 40,978gt, 40,560dwt), the OOCL *Fortune* was a sister ship to the OOCL *Freedom*. She was at Berth 204, Southampton, on 11 June 2000. Her status is now listed as 'dead' and she has been broken up. (Author collection)

The OOCL *Washington* (2010; 89,097gt, 99,631dwt; IMO 9417256) was at Southampton on the afternoon of 28 August 2011, alongside Berth 204. (Author collection)

A handsome ship, the OOCL *Nagoya* (2009; 40,168gt, 50,501dwt; IMO 9445538) was built by Samsung Shipbuilding and Heavy Industries (hull 1729). She is shown here at Berth 207 in Southampton on 13 November 2011. (Author collection)

Passing Calshot, inbound for Southampton on 29 September 2012, was the OOCL *Kaohsiung* (2006; 69,000dwt, 67,500gt; IMO 9307009). She had a maximum TEU capacity of 5,888 (3,944 at 14t). (Author collection)

A further view of the inbound OOCL *Kaohsiung* as she follows the buoyed Channel into Southampton. (Author collection)

Almost a contemporary of the OOCL *Nagoya*, the OOCL *Luxembourg* (2010; 89,097gt, 99,500dwt; IMO 9417270) was also a product of Samsung (hull 1722) and had a capacity of 6,274 TEUs at 14t. (S.C.H. Hucknall)

The NYK *Vesta* (2007; 97,825gt, 103,260dwt; IMO 9312808), photographed at Berth 205 at Southampton on 30 July 2012. Her container capacity is 7,000 TEUs at 14t (9,012 max.). (Author collection)

NYK *Hercules* (2013; 141,003gt, 144,400dwt; IMO 9622617) is owned by OOCL and was on charter to NYK when seen at Southampton on 6 June 2013. A good-looking vessel, it was built by Samsung Shipbuilding and Heavy Industries. She has a maximum TEU capacity of 13,000 (9,080 at 14t). She also has 800 reefer plugs. (Author collection)

Looking superb in the early March sun with her light grey hull and pale blue lettering, the NYK *Helios* (2013; 158,000gt, 142,400dwt; IMO 9622588) is seen at Berth 204/205 at Southampton. She was working Loop 4 on the Asia–Europe service of OOCL/ NYK. Her container capacity is 13,000 TEUs and 9,080 at 14t. (Author collection)

At the DP World Berth at Southampton, on 5 September 2013, was the NYK *Hermes* (2013; 158,000gt, 144,179dwt; IMO 9622631). She was the sixth unit out of ten neo-post-Panamax ships ordered by OOCL. NYK and OOCL are partners in the joint G6 Asia–Europe Network. (Author collection)

Formerly Hamburg Süd's *Cap Trafalgar* (1990; 29,739gt, 33,149dwt; IMO 8710950) with a capacity of 2,022 TEUs, the vessel retained her name until January 1999 when she became CMA CGM *Pasteur*. Here she is seen at Southampton. She is a small vessel compared to the current container carriers. (Author collection)

At Berth 204, Southampton, on 27 August 2011 was the CMA CGM *Andromeda* (2009; 131,332gt, 131,230dwt; IMO 9410727). She was deployed on the FAL 3 Asia–Europe service. Her capacity was 11,388 TEUs nominal (8,130 at 14t) with 800 reefer points. (Author collection)

Opposite top: Mid-afternoon at Berth 205, Southampton, saw the CMA CGM *Strauss* (2004; 65,427gt, 73,235dwt; IMO 9280641). Built by Samsung, she could carry 4390 TEU (14t). (Author collection)

Opposite bottom: Seemingly ignored by the fishermen, the CMA CGM *Titan* (2009; 131,332gt, 131,235dwt; IMO 9399222) is at Berth 204, Southampton. She was working on the FAL (French Asia Line) 3 service. Her maximum capacity is 11,312 TEU (8,900 at 14t) and she can also service 700 reefer containers. (Author collection)

A CMA CGM 'Explorer' class vessel, the *Alexander von Humboldt* (2013; 175,343gt, 186,470dwt; IMO 9454448) was formally named at Hamburg on 31 May 2013. Flying the UK flag, she has a capacity of 10,000 TEUs and is the second vessel of this size to be delivered to the company. On her way to Berth 207 at the same time was the CMA CMG *Chopin* (2004; 73,235dwt, 65,247 summer dwt; IMO 9280603). She worked within the Europe–Pakistan–India service. (Author collection)

Opposite top: Leaving Southampton for Antwerp on 3 January 2013, the NYK *Adonis* (2010; 98,800gt, 106,000dwt; IMO 9468293) was passing Calshot Spit. Built by IHI Corp. (Yard No. 3278), she has a maximum draught of 14m and a maximum TEU capacity of 9,600 and 800 reefer plugs. (Author collection)

Opposite bottom: Following the dredged Channel at Southampton on 24 March 2002 was P&O *Nedlloyd Southampton* (1998; 80,942gt, 88,669dwt; IMO 9153850). She was built at Kure by IHI Marine and is a post-Panamax vessel with a capacity of 6,674 TEUs (5,060 at 14t) and 710 reefers. (Author collection)

Inbound for Southampton is the P&O *Nedlloyd Stuyvesant* (2001; 80,654gt, 87,370dwt; IMO 9211482). Her maximum capacity is 6,802 TEUs (5,579 at 14t). She was built by Hyundai H.I., Ulsan (Yard No. 1274). She became the *Maersk Kingston* in 2006 and is now the *Maersk Klaipeda*. (Author collection)

On 16 October 2001, the P&O *Nedlloyd Houtman* (2001; 80,654gt, 87,370 dwt; IMO 9215311) was at Berth 205, Southampton. She was built by Hyundai H.I. (hull 1276) and has a capacity for 6,788 TEUs and has 710 reefer points. Renamed *Maersk Kampala*, she operates on the Europe–Far East service. (Author collection)

The container ship P&O *Nedlloyd Rotterdam* (1998; 88,669dwt; IMO 9153862) while at Southampton. The vessel has a capacity for 6,690 TEUs and 710 reefer connections. She is now named *Maersk Kalmar*. (Author collection)

Picking up speed off Calshot on 9 September 2001 was the P&O *Nedlloyd Jakarta* (1998; 31,333gt, 38,250 summer dwt; IMO 9168192). She was built by Kvaerner, Warnemünde, and had a modest capacity of 2,890 TEUs. (Author collection)

In January 1998, the NOL *Turquoise* (1996; 52,086gt, 60,323dwt; IMO 9082348) was alongside at Berth 205, Southampton. Owned by Neptune Ship Management, Bethesda, MD, she had a TEU capacity of 4,369 (max.) or 3,500 at 14t. Now operated by APL Bermuda Ltd, she has been renamed APL *Turquoise* and works the China–Australia service. (Author collection)

Regina Maersk (43,332gt, 53,310dwt; IMO 8300119) was built by Odeuse Steel Shipyard in 1983. She is shown at Berth 205 at Southampton on 11 July 1993. Behind the Bury Buoy, work was in progress on Berth 207 (420m long), which was brought into use in December 1996. (Author collection)

At 3 p.m. on 8 December 1998, the *Karen Maersk* (1996; 81,488gt, 82,135dwt; IMO 9085558) had left the container berth and was passing Mayflower Park at Southampton. Built by Odense Steel Shipyard, Odense (Yard No. 157), she was owned by Hammonia Rederei, Hamburg. Now renamed the *Maersk Karlskrona*, she has a maximum capacity of 7,908 TEUs. (Author collection)

For over thirty years, Hapag-Lloyd vessels have served Southampton. Here the company's *Hong Kong Express* (1995; 36,606gt, 45,362dwt; IMO 9104902) is being worked. Built by Hyundai H.I., she was designed to carry dangerous goods (IMO category A) if required. She was formerly *Northern Majesty*. (Author collection)

The latest *Hong Kong Express* (2013; 142,295gt, 142,018dwt; IMO 9501356) is seen here at Berth 205, Southampton. Built by Hyundai H.I., Ulsan (Yard No. 2244), her TEU capacity is 13,167 with 800 reefer plugs. (Author collection)

An earlier product of Hyundai H.I., Ulsan, Hapag-Lloyd's *Basle Express* (2010; 93,750gt, 103,646dwt; IMO 9450428) passes the Western Docks at Southampton. With a capacity of 8,750 TEUs (max.) (6,310 at 14t), a comparison with the *Hong Kong Express* indicates a significant increase in container capacity in three years. (Author collection)

Having arrived from Colombo on 16 May 2012, Hapag-Lloyd's container ship *Nagoya Express* (2010; 93,750gt, 103,646dwt; IMO 9450428) was at Berth 204/205 at Southampton. She initially carried the name *Basle Express*. (Author collection)

The *Kuala Lumpur Express* (2000; 54,437gt, 66,781dwt) was built by Hyundai H.I., Ulsan, and managed by Costmare Shipping Co. S.A. With a TEU capacity of 4,900, she was one of three such vessels. (Author collection)

On 4 October 2001 at Berth 204, a sister ship was Hapag-Lloyd's *Bremen Express* (2000; 54,465gt, 66,971dwt). Her TEU capacity was 4,890 and, with the building of a replacement vessel, she was renamed the *Seoul Express*. (Author collection)

The Panamanian-registered NYK *Aquarius* (2003; 75,484gt, 81,171dwt; IMO 9262704) was built by Ishikawajima H.I. Co. Ltd, Japan. Seen here at Berth 204/205, Southampton, on 2 January 2010, she had a container capacity of 4,986 TEUs (at 14t) and 550 reefer TEUs. (Michael McKenna)

A post-Panamax vessel, the *Kyoto Express* (2005; 93,750gt, 103,800dwt; IMO 9295256) was built by Hyundai H.I., Ulsan, and is seen here at Southampton at Berth 205. (Author collection)

Managed and owned by SOFAT, Kuwait, the *Malik Al Ashtar* (2012; 141,077gt, 145,527dwt; IMO 9525900) is registered in Valletta. Operated by UASC, her container capacity is 9,200 at 14t (13,296 max. TEUs) and 1,000 TEUs. Seen here on 8 July 2013, she is being assisted into the DP World Berth at Southampton by three Svitzer tugs. (Author collection)

Opposite top: Arriving in the late evening of 20 August 2012, the UASC *Jebel Ali* (2012; 141,077gt, 145,238dwt) is shown with the setting sun illuminating its starboard side. Astern is Hapag-Lloyd's *Hamburg Express* (2012, 142,029gt; 140,580dwt). Built by Hyundai, she has a container capacity of 13,092 TEU (max). The latter serves Loop 4 of the G6 alliance service. (Author collection)

Opposite bottom: A view of the *Hamburg Express* and the *Jebel Ali* from Eling, on 20 August 2012, shows the lights of the latter reflected in the creek. (Author collection)

This early evening view of the Tollerort Container Terminal, Hamburg, on 31 March 2012 shows K Line's vessel *Harbour Bridge* (2007; 98,747gt, 98,849dwt; IMO 9302152). She is a post-Panamax ship, built by IHI Marine Ltd, Kure. (Author collection)

Opposite top: American President Lines (APL) was founded in 1848. It is now a wholly owned subsidiary of Neptune Orient Line, based in Singapore. Seen at Southampton, the APL *Indonesia* (1996; 51,938gt, 60,219dwt; IMO 9103702) follows the Channel to Test Quays. Operated by APL on charter from Nedlloyd Linen, she was renamed ANL *Indonesia* in 2002 and sold in 2003 to become the *Maersk Darwin*. She was sold again to become the MSC *Darwin*. Her capacity is 3,124 TEUs (at 14t) and 250 reefer plugs. (Author collection)

Opposite bottom: Seen at Southampton on 6 September 2011 is the APL *Florida* (2008; 71,787gt, 72,912dwt). She was built at Koyo Dockyard, Mihara, and has a capacity of 6,350 TEUs (max.) and 586 reefer plugs. (Author collection)

On 18 April 2013 the APL *Temasek* (2013; 151,200gt, 150,974dwt; IMO 9631955) was at Berth 204, Southampton (max. draft 12.8m). Officially named in Singapore on 25 March 2013 by the wife of the Republic's president, this vessel had a maximum TEU capacity of 13,900 and was a product of Hyundai Samho H.I. Co. Ltd (Yard No. 5630). (Author collection)

Opposite top: A line of container ships at Southampton on 15 August 2011 had CMA CGM *Bellini* at Berth 207, Hapag-Lloyd's *Frankfurt Express* at 205 and the APL *Oregon* (2010; 71,787gt, 72,912dwt; IMO 9532783) at 204. Built at Koyo Dockyard, the latter's container capacity was 4,494 at 14t (max. 6,350) and 500 for reefer TEUs. (Author collection)

Opposite bottom: APL *Paris* (2012; 114,000gt, 120,000dwt) is shown at Southampton on 16 December 2012. A product of Daewoo Shipbuilding and Maritime Engineering (hull 4238) and formerly the APL *Uxbridge*, she had a maximum capacity of 9,850 TEUs (7,100 at 14t) and 700 reefer points. Her maximum draught is 14.5m. (Author collection)

Managed by Melford International Terminal, N.S., and owned by Offen Reederei, Hamburg, the *San Antonio* (2008; 22,914gt, 28,197dwt; IMO 9347267) was at the Burchardkai Container Terminal, Hamburg, on 14 July 2012. Built by Hyundai H.I., Mipo Dockyard, Ulsan, she was formerly the *Ibn Rushd*, a name she carried until July 2009. She now trades between Europe and Central America/West Indies. (Author collection)

The *Salam Panjang* (1978; 6,145gt, 7,727dwt; IMO 7705855) was built by Miho Shipyard, Shizuoka, Japan. She is shown here in Singapore Roads on 12 June 2001. Her status is now recorded as 'dead'. (Author collection)

The container feeder ship *Angela J* (1994; 3,804gt, 4,800dwt summer; IMO 9071076) has a capacity of 390 TEUs with 50 reefer plugs. She is being offered for sale at the time of writing. (S.C.H. Hucknall)

The *Margareta B* (1998; 3,999gt, 5,397dwt; IMO 9121883) is seen outbound on the Elbe on 30 March 2012 with a full load of containers. In September 2012, she was involved in the start of a CMA CGM service between Gothenburg, Oslo, Moss and Rotterdam. (Author collection)

Inbound for Hamburg, on 30 March 2012, was the London-registered feeder ship *Reinbek* (2005; 16,324gt, 16,000dwt; IMO 9313204). Built by Jos. L. Meyer, Papenberg, she was rated to Ice Class 1A and could accommodate 1,054 TEUs (14t) down to 597, depending on draft. (Author collection)

Henneke Rambow (2007; 9,981gt, 1,274dwt; IMO 9354430) built by J.J. Sietas Werft for the owners – Rambow Reederei. She served many European ports, including Brunsbüttel, Kiel, Gdansk and Hamburg. (Author collection)

Relatively small container ships, the *Lorraine* (2006; 27,786gt, 37,800dwt; IMO 9311763) and the *Hansa Rendsburg* (2000; 18,335gt, 23,992dwt; IMO 9155377) were moored out-of-work at Hamburg on the late afternoon of 16 September 2011. The *Lorraine* was owned by XT Management, Haifa, whilst the *Hansa Rendsburg* (ex CP *Jabiru, Direct Jabiru*) was owned and managed by the long-established company Leonhardt & Blumberg. (Author collection)

Proceeding down the Elbe on the morning of 17 July 2012, with the Airbus Deutschland plant on her port side, was the small container ship *Robert* (2006; 9,981gt, 11,257dwt). She was on a regular run that involved Hamburg, Gothenburg, Bremerhaven and Fredericia. (Author collection)

Opposite top: At the Burchardkai, Hamburg, on the morning of 14 July 2012, was the *Bianca Rambow* (2004; 9,981gt, 11,286dwt; IMO 9297591). (Author collection)

Opposite bottom: The container ship *Freya* (2000; 5,067gt, 6,850dwt; IMO 9219874) was heading down the Elbe on 17 July 2012, past the Airbus Deutschland plant. Built by J.J. Sietas Werft, Hamburg, a typical route would involve ports such as Stockholm, Aarhus and Bremerhaven. (Author collection)

The *Vega Stockholm* (2006; 7,464gt, 8,306 summer dwt; IMO 9358533) seen on 15 July 2011. She is sailing towards the container berths at Southampton. A product of Fujian Mawei Shipbuilding, Mawei, China, her regular route was Belfast–Southampton –Greenock–Dublin–Southampton. (Author collection)

Opposite top: Picking up speed as she proceeded down the Elbe was the container ship RBD *Dalmatia* (2007; 7,430gt, 8,400dwt; IMO 9339076). She has a TEU capacity of 698 (max.) or 436 at 14t. (Author collection)

Opposite bottom: The container ship *Enforcer* (2004; 7,642gt, 9,450dwt; IMO 9255737), owned by J.R. Shipping, Harlingen, is seen leaving Southampton on 2 August 2012. Having three holds, she can carry 225 TEUs in the hold and 525 on deck. She has a service speed of 18 knots. (Author collection)

On a pleasant afternoon in September 2012, Hamburg Süd's container ship *Rio Madeira* (2009; 69,000gt, 80,500dwt) was moored at Berth 207 at Southampton. She had a container capacity of 4,350 TEUs (at 14t) and 1,365 reefer TEUs. At the time she was a regular on the Le Havre–Southampton–New York run. (Author collection)

Opposite top: The *Hyundai Tenacity* (2012; 133,000gt, 142,500dwt; IMO 9475674) was moored at Berth 204/205 at Southampton on 5 July 2012. Owned by the Danaos Corporation, she began a twelve-year time charter at the outset. Her container capacity is 9,000 TEUs (at 14t). (Author collection)

Opposite bottom: Built at the Nagasaki Yard of Mitsubishi, the MOL *Courage* (2008; 86,692gt, 90,634 summer dwt; IMO 9321263) was originally named MOL *Comfort*. Seen at Southampton on 30 June 2012, her cargo capacity is 8,540 TEUs (nominal) with 630 reefer plugs. (Author collection)

Port-side to the Burchardkai Container Terminal, Hamburg, on 15 July 2012, was Hapag-Lloyd's *Montreal Express* (2003; 55,994gt, 47,754dwt; IMO 9253741). Registered in London, she could carry 4,402 TEUs and 311 reefer plugs. (Author collection)

Owned by the government of the People's Republic of China, China Ocean Shipping Company (COSCO) is China's shipping and logistics supplier. Seen here at the Tollerort Container Terminal, Hamburg, on 15 July 2012, is the COSCO *America* (2008; 114,394gt; IMO 9345427). Until 2011, she had carried the name *Hanjin Alexandria*. (Author collection)

Inbound for the container terminal at Southampton on 23 June 2012 was the OOCL *California* (1995; 66,046gt, 67,765dwt; IMO 9102289). With a cargo capacity of 4,312 nominal TEUs and 300 reefers, she was built by MHI, Nagasaki. OOCL vessels are invariably well presented and the general appearance of neglect on the hull of this vessel is surprising to say the least. (Author collection)

At Southampton Container Terminal on 18 June 2012 was the CMA CGM vessel *Laperouse* (2010; 152,991gt, 156,887dwt; IMO 9454412). An 'Explorer' Class vessel, the *Laperouse* was employed on the FAL 1 service. She was built by Daewoo Shipbuilding and Marine Engineering. (Author collection)

At Burchardkai, Hamburg, on 15 July 2012, was Hamburg Süd's container ship *Santa Cruz* (2011; 80,000gt, 90,000dwt; IMO 9444742). She was working on the Europe–South America service and has a nominal container capacity of 7,100 TEUs (5,450 at 14t) and 1,600 reefer plugs. (Author collection)

Opposite top: Owned by Hapag-Lloyd, Hamburg, the *Sofia Express* (2010; 93,750gt, 37,699 net RT (Registered Tonnage); IMO 9450404) was at Berth 205 at Southampton on 23 June 2012. Her container capacity at 14t is 6,570 TEUs and 700 reefer plugs. (Author collection)

Opposite bottom: At Berth 204/205 at Southampton on 30 May 2012 was Neptune Ship Management's vessel APL *Southampton* (2012, 128,929gt, 131,358dwt; IMO 9462017). Flying the Singapore flag, she was built by Daewoo Shipbuilding and Marine Engineering at Goeje, South Korea. (Author collection)

On her way down the Elbe, on the afternoon of 2 April 2012, was the CMA CGM *Turquoise* (2008; 50,500gt, 51,400dwt; IMO 9386471). Her cargo capacity was modest (4,308 TEUs (max.), 2,771 at 14t and 326 reefer plugs). (Author collection)

Opposite top: At the Tollerort Terminal, Hamburg, on 30 March 2012 was the container ship COSCO *Hellas* (2006, 109,149gt, 107,277dwt; IMO 9308510). Owned by Costamare Shipping and operated by COSCO, she was in port at Valencia at the time of writing. (Author collection)

Opposite bottom: A further view of the Tollerort Terminal on 31 March 2012 showed K Line's *Harbour Bridge* (2007; 98,747gt, 98,849dwt; IMO 9301252) with her port-side to the quay. Built by Ishikawajima Harima H.I., her container capacity is 9,040 TEUs (6,100 at 14t). (Author collection)

On the morning of 26 May 2013, the UK-flagged CMA CGM *Alexander von Humboldt* (2013; 153,022gt, 157,092dwt; IMO 9454448) was alongside at Southampton. Formerly named CMA CGM *Vasco da Gama*, she can carry 10,000 TEUs at 14t (16,020 max.) and has 1,100 reefer plugs. Parallel to her, another CMA CGM vessel *Chopin* (2004; 65,247gt, 73,235dwt; IMO 92806030)) was being manoeuvred. By comparison, the *Chopin* had a TEU capacity of 5,732 (4,390 at 14t and 632 reefer plugs). (Author collection)

Leaving Southampton, on the afternoon of 15 April 2013, was the APL-NOL vessel APL *Chongqing* (2011, 120,000dwt; IMO 9461867). Built by Hyundai Heavy Industries Ltd, her maximum container capacity is 10,070 TEUs (7,520 at 14t). She can also accommodate 700 reefer containers. (Author collection)

2

GENERAL CARGO SHIPS

Men at work on the *Apollogracht* (1991; 7,949gt, 12,150 summer dwt; IMO 9014896).
Built by Tille Scheepsbouw, Koostertille, she is a general cargo/heavy lift vessel with a
TEU capacity of 678. (Author collection)

Deck cargo (including containers and yachts) carried by the *Apollogracht* at Southampton on 12 May 2002 is shown. An officer stands on the bridge wing, overseeing cargo handling. (Author collection)

This impression of the newly developed Berth 201/202 at Southampton, currently under construction, superbly illustrates the changing scene in merchant shipping. It shows a very large vessel under the spreaders and three other vessels being worked at Berths 204–207. Away from the quaysides, vast numbers of containers await disposal, together with the large number of vehicles required for their distribution. (ABP Southampton)

Built by Rickmers Werft, Bremerhaven, the *Paul Rickmers* (1955; 7,802gt, 11,400 summer dwt; IMO 5272103) was owned by Rickmers Line. Seen here at Antwerp on 15 October 1980, she had been flagged out to Singapore in 1972. She was scrapped in 1982. (Author collection)

Passing Lonsdale Quay on her starboard side, the *Bremen Bridge* (2001; 66,800gt, 66,500dwt; IMO 9247546) was outward bound from Vancouver on 3 September 2010. Formerly YM *Bremen*, she has a capacity of 5,570 (max.) TEUs (4,170 at 14t). (Author collection)

Picking up speed past Stanley Park, Vancouver, the *Bremen Bridge* is about to pass under Lion's Gate Bridge and follow the Burrard Inlet to the sea. (Author collection)

The *Oakland* as she approaches Vancouver. In the background, North Vancouver can be seen. (Author collection)

The Open Hatch Cargo Carrier *Star Derby* (1979; 27,104gt, 43,700dwt; IMO 7700714) is seen at Squamish, British Columbia, in September 2010. Squamish is located at the north end of the Howe Sound, approximately 50 miles north of Vancouver. (Author collection)

Moored in the Burrard Inlet off North Vancouver, in September 2010, was the bulk carrier *Sealink Prosperity* (1984; 85,504gt, 160,993dwt; IMO 8319328). Built at MHI Nagasaki Shipyard and Engineering Works, she was formerly the *Orient Fortune*. (Author collection)

At Southampton's bulk quay, with the bunkering ship *Whitonia* alongside, is the *Anastasia S* (2004; 29,990gt, 52,808dwt; IMO 9277656). Registered in the Marshall Islands, she had been the *Electra* (until April 2005) and *Elect II* (until January 2007). (Author collection)

Owned by Temm Maritime, Kobe, the bulk carrier *Maple Island* (2012; 31,243gt, 55,610dwt; IMO 9478925) was loading scrap metal at Berth 107/108, Southampton, on 2 January 2012. (Author collection)

At Berth 205, Southampton, on the afternoon of 6 November 2011 was the CMA CGM *Strauss* (2004; 65,247gt, 73,235dwt; IMO 9280641). Built by Samsung Shipbuilding and Heavy Industries, she has a capacity of 4,390 TEUs (at 14 tons). (S.C.H. Hucknall)

A cold November day saw the container ship CMA CGM *Chopin* (2004; 65,730gt, 73,235dwt; IMO 9280603) Berth 205, Southampton. The vessel has a modest container capacity – 4,390 TEUs (at 14t) and 632 reefer TEUs. She is employed on the Asia–Europe service of the company. (Author collection)

At Southampton, at 7 p.m. on 21 February 2012, was the CMA CGM *Pelleas* (2008; 111,249gt, 120,853dwt; IMO 9365788). Operated by CMA CGM, the managing owner was Rederei Klaus-Peter Offen KG. (Michael McKenna)

Owned by Offen Klaus-Peter Rederei, the CMA CGM *Alaska* (2011; 158,000gt, 142,400dwt; IMO 9469572) had been initially named the CPO *Toulon*. With a capacity for 9,080 TEUs at 14t (12,562 TEUs max.) and 1,000 reefers, she was alongside Berth 204 at Southampton on 25 March 2013. (S.C.H. Hucknall)

At Southampton Container Terminal on the afternoon of 12 September 2013 was APL *Vanda* (2013; 151,963gt, 150,951dwt; IMO 9631993). Operated by Neptune Ship Management Services (the container shipping arm of Singapore's NOL Group), she works on the Asia–Europe Loop 7 service. She was the fifth out of ten 'megacarriers' capable of transporting 14,000 TEUs. (Author collection)

The cruise ship *Norwegian Breakaway* (2013; 144,017gt, 11,000dwt; IMO 9606912) was built by Meyer Neptun Werft and is the world's fifth-largest cruise ship. Seen here at Southampton on 30 April 2013 on her maiden voyage between Southampton and New York. The design on the front section of the vessel had been created by the artist Pelen Max. (Author collection)

At Berth 204 (max. draft 12.8m), on 18 April 2013, was APL *Temasek* (2013; 151,200gt, 150,974dwt; IMO 9631955). Officially named in Singapore on 25 March 2013 by the wife of the Republic's president, the vessel has a maximum TEU capacity of 13,900 and was a product of Hyundai Samho H.I. Ltd. (Author collection)

At Southampton on 18 May 2008 was the *Maersk Taikung* (2007; 94,193gt, 107,349dwt; IMO 9334662). Built by Daewoo Shipbuilding, she was described in the contemporary press as 'huge'. Compared to some of the present container ships, the description of her capacity (6,670 TEUs at 14t and 700 reefer plugs) would be scaled back, probably to 'large'. (Michael McKenna)

A superb photograph showing the OOCL *Seoul* (2010; 89,097gt, 99,655dwt; IMO 9417244) at Southampton on the evening of 21 February 2010. Built by Samsung Shipbuilding and Heavy Industries, her container capacity was 6,274 TEUs (at 14t) and 700 reefers. (Michael McKenna)

Registered in London, the CMA CGM *Gemini* (2010; 131,332gt, 131,230dwt) entered the port of Southampton on 6 September 2011. Her container capacity was 8,130 TEUs (at 14 tons) and 800 FEUs on deck. She is now used on the PEARL (South China–US West Coast) service. (Author collection)

Photographed at DP World, Vancouver, on 8 September 2010, the APL *Xiamen* (2001; 66,332gt, 67,170dwt) was waiting to be unloaded. Formerly the *Rotterdam Bridge* (until 2004), she became the YM *Rotterdam* and assumed her APL name in May 2010. (Author collection)

Owned by Columbus Ship Management GmbH and built by Flenderwerft-Lübeck (hull 652), the geared container ship *Cap Finisterre* (1991; 29,841gt, 33,221dwt; IMO 8710896) had a capacity of 2,032 TEUs and 267 reefer TEUs. She was moored at Berth 204, SCT, one evening in 2004. (Author collection)

The *Humboldt Rex* (1998; 7,637gt, 9,011 summer dwt; IMO 9179397) unloading her cargo of fruit at Berth 105, Southampton, on 27 November 2011. That season, she was a regular on the roundtrip to Tenerife. (S.C.H. Hucknall)

Assisted by Itchen Marine's tug *Wye Force*, the *Humboldt Rex* leaves Southampton. At the time she was involved in a regular run, carrying fruit from the Canary Islands to the South Coast. She retained her name until September 2012 and is now the *Aracena Carrier*. (Author collection)

The effects of a western maritime climate are clearly shown in this photograph of the Holland–America Line cruise ship *Rotterdam* (1997; 61,849gt, 6,354dwt; IMO 9122552). She was moored in the Burrard Inlet, Vancouver. (Author collection)

Seen at Lonsdale Quay, North Vancouver, in September 2010, is the chemical products tanker *Nordstrait* (2007; 30,068gt, 51,202 summer dwt). She is owned by Interorient Maritime Services GmbH & Co. KG. (Author collection)

The oil products tanker *Whitonia* (2007; 4,292gt, 7,511dwt; IMO 9342607) is owned by Whitaker Tankers, Hull. She was built by Dubai Dry Dock and is registered in the Isle of Man. She is seen here on the afternoon of 29 February 2012, heading towards Fawley. (Author collection)

A mid-sized cruise ship, P&O's *Aurora* (2000; 76,152gt, 8,486dwt; IMO 9169524) was built by Meyer Werft, Papenberg. P&O wanted the vessel to be built in the UK but at the time no British yard was large enough to fulfil the order. She is seen here at Southampton on 12 August 2011. (Author collection)

Just after 9 a.m. on 6 July 2013, the *Essen Express* (2013; 142,295gt, 142,022dwt; IMO 9501370) was manoeuvred into Berth 207, Southampton, by three Switzer tugs. (S.C.H. Hucknall)

Owned by Tesch Beredning and operated by CMA CGM, the *Alexander B* (ex-*Maersk Rundvik*) (2006; 14,072gt, 18,530dwt; IMO 9328646) has a TEU capacity of 915 at 14t and 178 reefer TEUs. She is on the River Elbe inbound for Hamburg, with the Airbus Deutschland factory at Finkenwerder astern on her starboard side. (S.C.H. Hucknall)

Launched on 21 March 2003, the *Queen Mary 2* (2003; 148,528gt, 19,189dwt) was named in 2004. She is the only Cunard transatlantic liner currently in service between Southampton and New York. She is seen here at her home port on 12 December 2011, with the former *Calshot Spit* light vessel in the foreground. (Author collection)

The NYK *Hermes* (2013; 141,003gt, 144,179dwt; IMO 9622631) is managed and owned by OOCL. She is the sixth unit in a series of neo-over Panamax ships ordered by OOCL. NYK and OOCL are partners in the joint G6 Asia–Europe network. She has a capacity of 9,080 TEUs (at 14t) and 800 reefer TEUs. (Author collection)

In the late evening of 20 August 2012, UASC's *Jebel Ali* (2012; 141,077gt, 145,238dwt) was moored at Berth 204/205 at Southampton. Her container capacity is 13,500 TEUs. She serves the AEC 2 service. Astern was Hapag-Lloyd's *Hamburg Express*. (Author collection)

Built by Frisian Shipbuilding, Welgelegen, the *Edisongracht* (1994; 8,448gt, 12,760 summer dwt; IMO 9081289) multi-purpose cargo vessel is seen at the Eastern Docks, Southampton. Her ownership seems to alternate between Spliethoffs and Nanavut Eastern Arctic Shipping, Montreal. (Author collection)

Operated by Spliethoffs BV, the general cargo vessel *Saimaagracht* (2005; 18,321gt, 23,660dwt; IMO 9288069) has container-carrying facilities (1,291 TEUs (max.) capacity). Seen at Southampton at the former Berth 202 (now under redevelopment) on 1 September 2011, she was in the Gulf of Mexico at the time of writing. (Author collection)

Moored at Berth 108 (the former bulk terminal) at Southampton in the early 2000s was the *Arklow Dawn* (1982; 7,944gt, 20,780dwt). She was originally the *Falknes* (ex-*Fitnes*, *Falknes* (again), *Uri* and *Daisy Green*). (Author Collection)

Built in 2007, the general cargo ship *Normed Rotterdam* (8,407gt, 11,145 summer dwt) was managed by Universal Marine BV – Krimpen aan den Ijssel. With a deck cargo of pressure vessels, she was seen at Berth 202, Southampton, on 23 August 2012. (Author collection)

The days of the conventional cargo vessel have probably gone. Here, *Captain Christos* (1976; 7,345gt, 11,775 summer dwt; IMO 7610787) was leaving Southampton on 4 November 2000. Over its career, it carried many names (*Mary Gold, Artemis, Yue Hope*) but finally became *Captain Mustafa*, owned by SS Maritime Majuro, Marshall Islands, and flying the Togolese flag. (Author collection)

At Berth 103 at Southampton, on 18 June 2000, was the multi-purpose vessel *Iran Kordestan* (1999; 16,694gt, 23,176 summer dwt; IMO 9167265). Owned by Rahbaran Omid Darya Ship Management, Teheran, she had four 30-ton cranes and a capacity for 970 TEUs and 42 reefer points. The vessel was renamed *Sea State* in November 2008 and the *Lilied* (until July 2011). She may now be the Moldovan *Gloxinia*. (Author collection)

With the old grain silos in the Eastern Docks at Southampton in the background, the general dry cargo ship *Arni 1* (1972; 4,782gt, 6,274dwt) is seen. A type 96 vessel, built in East Germany, she had been the *Volodya Shcherbatsevich* and was registered in Batumi in the Republic of Georgia. (Author collection)

The general cargo ship *Andrea Brovig* (1979; 9,696gt; IMO 7712169), formerly *Capitaine Wallis II*, was in Singapore Roads in June 2001. She is currently owned by Neptune Shipping of Port Vila. (Author collection)

Alongside Berth 103/104 at Southampton on 23 May 2011, the Spliethoffs Bevrachtingskantoor vessel *Snoekgracht* (2000; 16,641gt, 21,402dwt) was unloading deck cargo using her own gear. She had arrived overnight from Newport, Rhode Island and left for Eemshaven late the following day. (Author collection)

Built by Scheepswerven, Bodewes, Hoogezand, the general cargo ship *Vedette* (1990; 2,033gt, 3,502dwt; IMO 8909185) was owned by Beck's. Sold in 2005 to Faversham Ships, she retained her name. (Author collection)

3

RO-ROS

In dry dock at Falmouth on 30 July 1991, was the Ro-Ro cargo vessel *Stena Dan* (1988; 19,683gt, 13,925dwt; IMO 8501476). Apparently still active, she appears to be the India-registered *Navdenhu Swift* owned by Arcadi Shipping, Mumbai. (Author collection)

In dock at Falmouth on 10 August 1994 was the CGM *Renoir* (1979; 32,498gt, 22,138dwt; IMO 7504598). She had been built as *Renoir* by Chantier de l'Atlantique (Alstholm), St Nazaire. Its subsequent history is confusingly reported but it seems to have been converted to a livestock carrier in 1998. (Author collection)

At Berth 43, Southampton, on 20 October 2001, was the Wilhelmsen Ro-Ro *Tourcoing* (1978; 22,434gt, 33,718dwt; IMO 7705946). She was modified in April 2004 by the installation of a car and truck garage on the weather deck. She was sold in May 2010 for breaking in China. (Author collection)

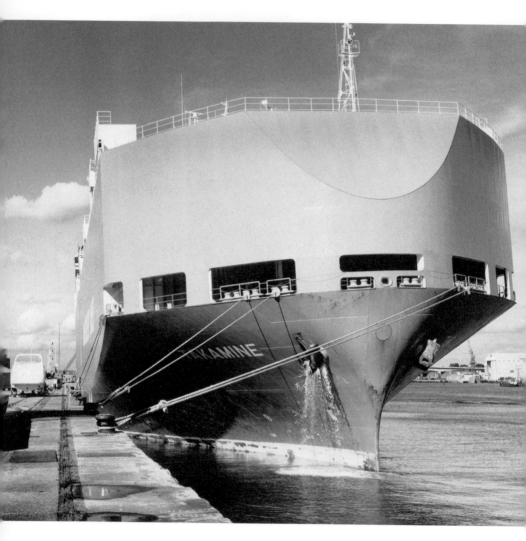

The Wilhelmsen Ro-Ro *Takamine* (1997; 49,821gt, 19,884dwt; IMO 9129706) was built by Sumitomo H.I., Yokosuko (hull 1215). She is seen here at Berth 34/35, Southampton, on 29 September 2001. Sold in November 2003, she was renamed *Freedom* by her owners, ARC (American Roll-on Roll-off Carriers). (Author collection)

The Ro-Ro *Tapiola* (1978; 22,325gt, 33,702dwt; IMO 7705934) was launched as the *Boogabilla* for Rederi Aktie Bolagete Transatlantic, Sweden. Seen here at the Itchen Quays, Southampton, in her original condition, she was rebuilt in 2004 when the container space was replaced by extra car decks. She was laid up in March 2010. (Author collection)

At the original Berth 202, Southampton (before the present development), the PCTC *Trinidad* (1987; 49,750gt, 15,529dwt (max. draft)) is shown. With thirteen decks (four hoistable), she has a capacity for 6,050 units or 620 trucks. (Author collection)

Opposite: Loading at Southampton for Baltimore, on 5 August 2001, was the Ro-Ro vessel *Tampere* (1989; 22,087gt, 35,098dwt). Her container capacity was 1,814 TEUs. Launched for Brostroms Rederi A/B, Sweden, she was bought by Tampere Shipping A/S and its owners became Wilhelmsen Lines A/S. (Author collection)

The Wilhelmsen vehicle carrier *Taronga* (1996; 72,709gt, 48,988dwt; IMO 9121273) is shown loading vehicles at Southampton on 23 June 2002. She is now the *Endurance*, owned by American Ro-Ro Carrier (ARC) of Parkridge, New Jersey. (Author collection)

Moored at Berth 35, Southampton, on 17 March 2002, was the vehicle carrier *Don Juan* (1995; 55,598gt, 15,199dwt). Managed and owned by Wallenius Maritime, she is registered in Singapore. (Author collection)

The PCTC *Turandot* (1995; 55,598gt, 22,815dwt) is seen alongside Berth 35 at Southampton in 2002. Her vehicle capacity is 2,960 cars and 490 trucks or 5,846 cars. (Author collection)

A view of Berth 41, Southampton, showing the RoRo (PCTC) *Maersk Wind* (1990; 51,770gt, 16,886 summer dwt; IMO 9185463) and Spliethoff's *Achtergracht* at Berth 39. Currently, the PCTC is named *Hoegh Osaka*. (Author collection)

At Berth 41 on 1 September 2001 was the vehicle carrier *Maersk Wave* (2000; 51,770gt, 16,919dwt; IMO 9185451). (Author collection)

Opposite top: Berth 34 at the Eastern Docks in Southampton, on 27 August 2001, was occupied by Wallenius Wilhelmsen's *Tellus* (1978; 47,089gt, 17,406dwt; IMO 7518563). A vehicle carrier, she retained her name until August 2003, when she became ARC's *Independence* – a name she carried until April 2008. (Author collection)

Opposite bottom: Following the Channel at Southampton was the Ro-Ro passenger ship *Repubblica di Amalfi* (1989; 42,574gt, 25,450dwt; IMO 8521218). She had a maximum capacity of 116 TEUs and 40 reefer points. Last reported in Malta in September 2012, her present status is 'dead'. (Author collection)

Seen here at the Eastern Docks, Southampton, the Ro-Ro vehicle carrier *Aquarius Leader* (1998; 57,623gt, 22,815dwt; IMO 9158276) was managed by NYK for Hercules Ship Management plc Ltd. (Author collection)

Opposite top: Inbound at Hamburg on 4 April 2012 was the Ro-Ro cargo vessel *Grande Benin* (2009; 47,120gt, 26,097dwt; IMO 9343170). She was one of a series of seven multi-purpose Ro-Ros built for Grimaldi. (Author collection)

Opposite bottom: The Solent pilot, accompanied by a crew member, boards Wallenius' *Otello* (1992; 52,479gt) on 20 July 2002. Sold in 2005 and renamed *Integrity*, Wallenius took delivery of a new *Otello* in 2006. (Author collection)

With the oil products tanker *Jaynee W.* (1996; 1,689gt, 2,901dwt) in attendance, the Wallenius-Wilhelmsen PCTC *Aida* was alongside Berth 201/202. She had been built by Daewoo H.I. Ltd, Korea, and had a capacity for 6,700 cars or 3,000 cars and 100 buses. (Author collection)

Opposite top: The Ro-Ro vessel *Asian Chorus* (1977; 55,729gt, 21,505 summer dwt; IMO 9158604) was managed and owned by Haeyoung Maritime Services, Panama. (Author collection)

Opposite bottom: Assisted by the tug *Brightwell*, Wallenius' vehicle carrier *Don Carlos* (1997; 67,141gt, 28,142dwt; IMO 9122655) was leaving the Eastern Docks, Southampton, on 23 June 2002. (Author collection)

Wallenius-Wilhelmsen's *Toba* (1979; 22,008gt, 34,310dwt) could carry 1,806 TEUs and 3,832 cars. She is seen here at Berth 40, Southampton, on 4 June 2002. In 2003, the vessel was rebuilt as a car carrier and transferred to Mk I Shipping Pte, Singapore (50/50 ownership). In 2009, the *Toba* (and *Tapiola*) were laid up in Lyngal, Norway, due to a recession-induced slump in automotive sales and, thereby, a decline in the transport of cars and Ro-Ro cargo. Her status now is 'dead'. (Author collection)

Opposite top: At Berth 41, Southampton, in May 2012 was the vehicle carrier *Dover Highway* (2011; 59,030gt, 18,720dwt; IMO 9574107). She was owned by Taiyo Nippon Kisen-Kobe. (Author collection)

Opposite bottom: Wallenius' PCTC *Don Carlos* (1997; 28,141dwt; IMO 9122655) is being manoeuvred towards the Itchen Quays at Southampton. With thirteen car decks, she had a maximum capacity of 5,873 cars or 2,949 cars and 488 trucks. She was later chartered to Bukor, Serbia. (Author collection)

Wilhelmsen's *Tarago* (2000; 67,140gt, 39,444dwt (max. draft); IMO 9191321) was a Mk IV Wilhelmsen Ro-Ro (35 per cent more covered capacity for specialised cargo than Mk III). Loading at Berth 35/36, Southampton, for St Johns, she was suitable for cars, trucks and equipment for construction and agriculture. (Author collection)

The vehicle carrier *Hoegh Osaka* (2000; 51,770gt, 16,886 summer dwt; IMO 9185463) was owned by Hoegh Autoliners, Oslo, and was managed by A.P. Møller. She is seen here on 29 September 2012 passing Calshot, having left Southampton's Eastern Docks. (Author collection)

4

BULK CARRIERS

Not the expected size of a bulk carrier, Jebsen's *Telnes* (1982; IMO 8001024) was a self-discharging bulk carrier, type 360. Built by Kvaerner Kleven M/V A/S, Ulsteinvik, she is shown leaving Southampton on 25 February 2001. From 1997 to 2003 she was owned by Telnes Panama B/V. (Author collection)

Leaving Hamburg and passing the Burchardkai Container Terminal, on 14 July 2012, was *Nord Aquarius* (2011; 45,250gt, 81,838dwt; IMO 9526485). Then sailing under the Singapore flag, she is now named *Trade Vision* and flying the Marshall Islands' flag. (Author collection)

Opposite top: In Queen Elizabeth No. 2 Dry Dock, Falmouth, was a typical 1950–60s bulker. Possibly a Dillingham Jebsen 'Birknes' Class vessel, she may have been the *Bergnes* (IMO 7380461). In the adjacent No. 1 Dock was the *Cape Palmas* (1960; 9,861gt, 17,029 summer dwt; IMO 5018387). The *Cape Palmas* retained her name until 10 January 1978, but the last photograph of her seems to have been at Sault Ste Marie in 1975. (George Harrison/author collection)

Opposite bottom: A present-day bulk carrier, the *K Coral* (2010; 32,839gt, 58,015dwt; IMO 9586708) was at Berth 108/107 at Southampton on the afternoon of 1 September 2011. One year later, on 4 October 2012, she was abandoned by her owners at Newcastle, New South Wales. (Author collection)

At Berth 107/108 at Southampton, on 6 August 2012, was the bulk carrier *DK Ione* (2010; 34,349gt, 58,714dwt; IMO 9528158). Alongside the vessel, Whitaker's oiler *Whitonia* was moored. (Author collection)

Opposite top: On 29 September 2012, a forest-product carrier (woodchip carrier), *Glorious Hibiscus* (2012; 49,097gt, 60,411 summer dwt; IMO 9515216), was at Berth 107/108, Southampton. The vessel was managed by NYK, Tokyo. (Author collection)

Opposite bottom: Owned by the Norwegian company Greig Shipping, the bulk carrier *Star America* (1985; 20,929gt, 30,168 summer dwt; IMO 8508280) was moored at Squamish, British Columbia, in September 2010. Squamish is a pleasant little town, approximately 50 miles north of Vancouver, on the Howe Sound. (Author collection)

The bulk carrier *Mimosa Dream* (1996; 40,169gt, 48,309dwt; IMO 9140566) is seen at Southampton at Berth 107/108 on 23 June 2012. (Author collection)

On its journey to the bulk quays at Vancouver, the *Oakland* (2000; 14,527gt, 23,622dwt) is seen passing under Lion's Gate Bridge, following the Burrard Inlet, in early September 2010. (Author collection)

5

REEFERS

Owned by Star Reefers, Gdynia, the *Regal Star* (1993; 10,375gt, 10,520dwt; IMO 9053658) is seen approaching the Western Docks, Southampton. Formerly the *Chiquita Tauu* (until 1994), *Hornstrait* (until 1995) and *Tauu* (until 1997), she proceeds to the Windward Terminal, Southampton. (Author collection)

Sometime later, the *Regal Star* is seen on her berth at the Windward Terminal, Southampton. (Author collection)

Opposite: Seen in dry dock at Falmouth in the summer of 1994 is the reefer *Akademik Vavilovs* (1985; 9,552gt, 7,673 summer dwt). Built at Danyard, Aalborg, Denmark, she was last reported in April 2012 at Port Said. Her present status is assumed 'dead'. (Author collection)

Leaving Hamburg in May 2012 was the *Pacific Mermaid* (1992; 9,820gt, 10,461dwt; IMO 9045924). The vessel has her own lifting gear (two 30mt and two 10mt cranes). Seen here with a good load of containers, her capacity is 140 TEUs and 13 FEUs (Forty foot Equivalent Units). She also has 65 reefer plugs. (Author collection)

Opposite: In a further view, the *Akademik Vavilovs* (1985; 9,552gt, 7,673 summer dwt) is seen alongside Berth 102, Southampton, in 2001. She was taking fuel from the Whitaker oiler *Jaynee W*. (Author collection)

One of four banana boats operating on the Southampton to Belize and Honduras weekly service that was in operation in the early 2000s, Star Reefers' vessel *English Star* is seen moored at Berth 107. The vessel was sold for scrapping in autumn 2011. (Author collection)

Owned by Honma Senpaku Tokyo and managed by BaltMed Reefer Services, the *Chikuma Reefer* (1998; 7,367gt, 8,097dwt; IMO 9184336) is seen leaving Southampton. She was employed at the time on a regular service between the port and the Canary Islands. (Author collection)

The fruit carrier *Solent Star* (2001; 10,804gt, 9,709dwt; IMO 9206061) was at the Windward Terminal at Southampton on 25 February 2001. She was managed and owned by Star Reefers, Gdynia. Built in Japan, she was registered in Monrovia. At the time, Star Reefers had a very modern fleet of ships. (Author collection)

At the Windward Terminal, Southampton, on 3 September 2000 was the *Southampton Star* (1999; 10,804gt, 9,709dwt; IMO 9206059). Owned by Star Reefers, Gdynia, she carried 306 TEUs. (Author collection)

6

PASSENGER SHIPS

In dry dock at Falmouth in the early 1990s was RMS *St Helena* (1990; 6,767gt, 3,130dwt; IMO 8716306). On 25 August 2013, the vessel made her final sailing from the UK. (Author collection)

In 1962, an unusual vessel joined the Royal Viking fleet. She was named *Royal Viking Queen* (1992; 9,961gt, 790 summer dwt; IMO 9008598) but had been designed to Seabourne Cruises' specifications. She is seen here at Falmouth on 12 August 1993. (Author collection)

A further view of the *Royal Viking Queen*. (Author collection)

Described as a 'beautiful ship', the *Sea Princess* was built by John Brown & Co. in 1966 as the *Kungsholm* for the Swedish–American Line. Bought by P&O in 1979 and renamed *Sea Princess*, she is seen at Southampton in P&O's colours. She was sold in 2002 to Leonardo Shipping and was laid up in 2010. (Author collection)

P&O's *Oriana* (1995; 69,153gt; IMO 9050137) was built by Jos. L. Meyer, Papenburg. She is seen here at City Cruise Terminal, Southampton. (Author collection)

The cruise ship *Artemis* (1984; 44,348gt, 5,580dwt; IMO 8201480) was built by Wärtsila, at Helsinki. She was named by Diana, Princess of Wales, on 15 November 1984 in Southampton, in the presence of the President of Finland. She retained her name until 2005, when she was sold to P&O and renamed. In 2011 she was sold to Phoenix Reisen, registered in Bermuda and renamed *Artenia*. (Author collection)

Leaving Southampton on 1 June 2013 was the *Independence of the Seas* (2008; 154,407gt, 10,600dwt; IMO 9349681). She was built by Aker Yards, Turku, Finland. (Author collection)

Much to the delight of the citizens of Hamburg, the Cunarders *Queen Elizabeth* and *Queen Mary* were in the port together on 15 July 2012. Shown here at 10.17 a.m. is the *Queen Elizabeth* (2010; 90,901gt, 7,685dwt). She was built by Fincantieri, Monfalcone, Italy (Yard No. 6187). (Author collection)

P&O Cruises' ship *Andonia* (2001; 30,277gt, 2,700dwt; IMO 9210220) was built by Chantiers de l'Atlantique, Nantes St Nazaire. She is managed and owned by Carnival UK. Her former names were *R Eight* (until March 2003), *Minerva II* (until March 2007) and *Royal Princess* (until April 2011). She is seen here at Southampton on 1 June 2013. (Author collection)

7

TUGS

Red Funnel Towage's tug *Redbridge* (1995; 339gt) assisting the *Regal Star* to berth at the Windward Terminal at Southampton on 8 October 2000. The *Redbridge* was renamed *Adstream Redbridge* in 2005 and *Svitzer Redbridge* in 2008. (Author collection)

Built by Yorkshire Dry Dock Co., Hull, the *Redbridge* was owned originally by the Southampton, Isle of Wight and South of England Steam Packet Co. She is seen here assisting P&O's *Oriana* at Southampton on 9 July 2000. (Author collection)

Opposite: A further view of the *Redbridge* as she approaches the *Oriana*, moored at Berth 40/41, Southampton, on 9 July 2000. (Author collection)

Assisted by Red Funnel Towage's tugs *Hamtun* and *Lyndhurst*, the banana boat *Crystal Prince* (1992; 7,743gt, 7,726 summer dwt; IMO 8912120) is shown leaving Berth 101/102 at Southampton. At the time, berth this served as the Windward Terminal. (Author collection)

Opposite: The Falmouth Towing Co.'s tugs *St Piran* and *St Mawes* were among a small group of tugs awaiting their next duty at Falmouth. (Author collection)

On the afternoon of 27 August 2011, the *Svitzer Bristol* was assisting the *Zim Rio Grande* in the upper swinging ground at Southampton. At the time, the *Zim* ship was a regular on the Le Havre–Southampton–New York run. (Author collection)

Opposite top: The *Svitzer Alma*, formerly *Lady Alma* (1996; 396gt, 320dwt; IMO 9141144) is seen carrying out her duties in the Bury Reach at Southampton. (Author collection)

Opposite bottom: Assisting in the berthing of the CMA CGM *Strauss*, at Southampton on 18 June 2012, is the tractor tug *Svitzer Bristol* (2003; 366gt, 210dwt; IMO 9280005). Built originally for service at Avonmouth Docks, she is owned by Svitzer Marine Ltd. Svitzer are part of the A.P. Møller Group. (Author collection)

Job completed, the *Svitzer Bentley* (1996; 381gt, 200dwt; IMO 9127356) pauses in the River Test on 30 April 2013. Her duty had been provision of assistance to the CMA CGM *Christophe Colombe* as she left Southampton. (Author collection)

Opposite top: With the assistance of a Svitzer tug, a well-laden NYK vessel is shown passing Mayflower Park, Southampton. (Author collection)

Opposite bottom: Proceeding down the River Elbe at Hamburg, on 31 March 2012, is the tug *Bugsier 18* (240gt, 113 summer dwt; IMO 9036246). She was built by PS Werften Wolgast, Volgast. (Author collection)

The *Svitzer Bristol* is seen here assisting with the berthing of the CMA CGM *Strauss* at Southampton Container Terminal. (Author collection)

8

TANKERS

Seen on the River Tyne at North Shields in the mid-1960s are the BP tanker *British Commerce* (1965; 37,800gt, 67,689dwt) and the Shell (UK) tanker *Daphnella* (1966; 39,929gt, 66,802dwt). (Author collection)

Shown at the Fawley Oil Refinery on 22 September 2012 is the crude-oil carrier *Stena Antarctica* (2006; 61,371gt, 114,849dwt; IMO 9322827). She is managed by Northern Marine Management, Clydebank. (Author collection)

Opposite top: At Falmouth, on 12 August 1993, was the replenishment vessel USNS *Paul Buck* (1985; 21,471gt, 35,572 summer dwt; IMO 8220773). Paul Buck had been the captain of the American Liberty ship *Stephen Hopkins*, which sank the German raider *Stier*. Buck was honoured in 1944 with a posthumous Merchant Marine DSM. The USNS *Paul Buck* was taken out of service and struck in 2010. (Author collection)

Opposite bottom: The Norwegian crude-oil tanker *Kronviken* (1988; 79,554gt, 152,423dwt; IMO 8613853) was owned by Viken Ship Management. She is seen here passing Calshot on her way to Fawley, accompanied by the tug *Thrax* (1994; 530gt), operated by Solent Towage. (Author collection)

The oil-product tanker *Whitchallenger* (2012; 2,958gt, 4,350dwt, 4,498 summer dwt; IMO 9252278) is shown at Southampton. She has a double hull and can carry heavy fuel oil, gas oil and lubricants. (Author collection)

The crude-oil and product tanker *Paramount Helsinki* (2010; 62,851gt, 114,165dwt; IMO 9453963) is an Aframax tanker with a double hull. Here, she is seen at Fawley on 3 January 2013. (Author collection)

The *Navion Britannia* (1998; 72,732gt, 126,650dwt; IMO 9145188) is a crude-oil tanker. She was at the Fawley Oil Refinery on 3 January 2013. (Author collection)

At the old Northumberland Dock is BP Tanker Co. Ltd's *British Commerce* (1965; 68,77dwt) being cleaned at the tanker-cleaning berth in May 1966. (Author collection)

LPG tanker *Thresher* (2007; 2,294gt, 4,750dwt; IMO 9377951) passing Calshot in August 2013. She has loaded at Fawley and is returning to the Netherlands. (Author collection)